GW01057410

Original title:
Otter Joy

Editor: Jessica Elisabeth Luik
Author: Lan Donne
ISBN HARDBACK: 978-9916-86-445-6
ISBN PAPERBACK: 978-9916-86-446-3

Wave Waltz

The ocean whispers soft and sweet,
A dance of calm beneath our feet.
The moonlight casts a silver hue,
As waves embrace the twilight blue.

Each crest and trough with rhythm sways,
A fluid waltz, the sea obeys.
Stars above both large and small,
Guide the dancers, one and all.

Strands of pearls in ocean's deep,
In secrets, they forever keep.
The tide's embrace, a lover's kiss,
In wave's embrace, eternal bliss.

Brookside Banter

By the brook, the whispers flow,
Chattering where the wildflowers grow.
Pebbles smooth from ages past,
Tell tales old, that ever last.

The water's song both clear and bright,
Catches the sun in dancing light.
With every twist and playful turn,
Stories from its depths we learn.

Frogs among the reeds do croak,
Adding cheer to nature's joke.
Leaves above, a green pavilion,
Shade the brook, a leafy million.

Playful Paws

In grassy fields where sunlight beams,
Kittens prance in joyful dreams.
Tiny paws in frolic play,
Chasing shadows through the day.

Whiskers twitch and tails held high,
Beneath the vast and open sky.
Butterflies in lazy flight,
Catch their eyes with pure delight.

Rolling, tumbling, full of cheer,
Every moment, no hint of fear.
Life's adventure in each pounce,
Joyful leaps that spring and bounce.

Meadow Mischief

Fields of green alive with glee,
Nature's actors wild and free.
Playful rabbits dashing by,
Underneath the azure sky.

Foxes dart in cunning chase,
A merry jaunt, a lively race.
Birds on wing with songs so sweet,
Join the chorus, upbeat, neat.

In the tall grass, secrets hide,
Where mischief makers come alive.
Dance of life from dawn till dusk,
In meadow's heart, a lively musk.

Mystical Marshlands

In the glow of twilight's gown,
Swamps arise with secrets deep.
Whispers in the cattails found,
Dreams awaken from their sleep.

Swaying reeds in silent dance,
Frogs serenade at dusk's embrace.
Moonlight casts a curious glance,
Over nature's hidden face.

Lilies glow with soft lament,
Ripples tell of ancient tales.
Echoes of the night are sent,
As the swamp's enchantment sails.

Water's Whimsy

Rivulets weave a path so bright,
Beneath the dappled canopy's light.
Glistening streams in pure delight,
Flowing free from dawn to night.

Pebbles, polished by the flow,
Tell a story all their own.
Each bend where wildflowers grow,
Holds whimsey in its tone.

Dancing drops on mossy green,
Sparkles in the noonday sheen.
Nature's laughter, soft yet keen,
In the brook, such joy is seen.

Dusk Delights

Evening drapes its gentle veil,
Shadows cast a muted spell.
Birds sing songs of nightfall's tale,
In the twilight's soft farewell.

Lantern bugs with tiny gleam,
Paint the dusk with fleeting light.
Silent as a tender dream,
Whispers blend with coming night.

Stars peek from the velvet veil,
Calm horizons stretch and lean.
In the hush where secrets sail,
Dusk delights in shades serene.

Feathered Friends

On wings of silk, the sparrows glide,
Across the azure, far and wide.
Songs of morning they confide,
In the golden beams they ride.

Robins, thrushes, in the trees,
Fill the air with melodies.
In their notes, the heart finds ease,
Underneath the rustling leaves.

Chickadees in playful flight,
Flit through branches' morning light.
Feathered friends, a pure delight,
In their song, day's new invite.

Joy on the Rocks

Waves crash on ancient stones,
Echoing time's embrace.
Laughter mingles with the foam,
In this treasured, sacred place.

Children dance on granite shores,
Feet splashing in the spray.
Birds sing from lofty oars,
As sun brings a golden day.

Seagulls soar in azure skies,
Freedom in their flight.
Pebbles catch the light that vies,
To sparkle, pure and bright.

Whispers in the salty breeze,
Stories old and new.
Nature's symphony, the keys,
Unlocking joy in view.

Tides that shape our fleeting time,
Mold joy with tender care.
Each wave a gentle rhyme,
Of moments we all share.

Liquid Laughter

Ripples dance in circles wide,
Laughter skips the stone.
Reflecting in the riverside,
The joy that we've all known.

Children's giggles fill the air,
Echoes of the streams.
Nature's laughter everywhere,
Mirroring our dreams.

Water's song, a merry tune,
In currents swift and light.
Underneath the harvest moon,
It sparkles through the night.

Liquid laughter, pure delight,
In every pool and pond.
Sharing moments of the bright,
And forging tender bonds.

Streams weave tales of mirth and glee,
In bubbly, chuckling flow.
Nature joins in harmony,
With laughter that we sow.

Aquatic Playground

Leaping fish in water clear,
Joyful splashes high.
Lilies bloom in waves sincere,
Beneath the azure sky.

Turtles bask on sunlit logs,
Watching shadows play.
Frogs leap from the reedy bogs,
In this aquatic fray.

Dragonflies in shimmering flight,
Skim the liquid stage.
Nature's ballet, pure delight,
In timeless, ageless age.

Children's feet find sandy ground,
In this playful scene.
Splashing waters all around,
In endless, summer sheen.

Bubbles rise to meet the sun,
In joyous, sparkling ride.
Aquatic games, where we become,
One with the flowing tide.

Glistening Games

Sunlight dances on the crest,
Of waves that kiss the shore.
Children join in nature's jest,
In games that we adore.

Glistening sands, a treasure trove,
Beneath our seeking toes.
Each step a delicate wove,
Of secrets only water knows.

Seaglass gems and shells so bright,
Bid us to explore.
In this game of pure delight,
There's always something more.

Echoes of our gleeful cries,
Blend with ocean's song.
Beneath the broad and open skies,
Where we find we belong.

In glistening games, hearts alight,
With joy that never fades.
As day turns gently into night,
Our memories it shades.

Cheerful Channels

In bright, meandering streams so pure,
Laughter dances, hearts allure.
Sunswept ripples, joys convey,
Flowing free, in endless play.

Whispers of a sunshine tune,
Merriment beneath the noon.
Streams of cheer, like golden rays,
Guide the soul through dazzling days.

Songs of water, crisp and clear,
Carry dreams to catch and steer.
Buoyant bubbles, spirits rise,
Underneath the azure skies.

Leaves and petals on the go,
Ride the currents soft and slow.
Happy travels, onward gleam,
In those cheerful channels' beam.

Beneath the Surface

Deep below the tranquil waves,
Hidden realms the water paves.
Secrets, silent, resting there,
In the depths, far from despair.

Underneath the mirrored sheen,
Life emerges, unpredicted, unseen.
Mysteries flourish, shadows play,
Where light and dark in cycles sway.

Ancient echoes whisper low,
Within currents, silence flows.
Creatures, unseen tales they weave,
In the deep, where dreams conceive.

Through the veil of crystal hues,
Mystic wonders, soulful clues.
Beneath the surface, truths reside,
In the stillness, there they hide.

Brimming Banks

Where rivers kiss the verdant shore,
Nature's voice begins to roar.
Life abounds in lush embrace,
At the banks, the wild chase.

Dew-kissed grass and whispered breeze,
Crimson flowers, swaying trees.
Brimming banks, a world unfurled,
Magic brushes, colors swirled.

Dragonflies in sunlight's beam,
Flutters weave a living dream.
Songs of earth and sky converge,
At the edge, where spirits merge.

Ripples meet with open arms,
Nurturing with endless charms.
Brimming banks, a harmony,
Nature's tender, sweet decree.

Splashing Spirits

In the brook's lively embrace,
Spirits dance in joyous grace.
Splashing droplets, laughter's sound,
Nature's pulse, where hearts rebound.

Children's giggles, waters play,
Echoes of a carefree day.
Sunlit sprays in wild flight,
Catch the beams, ignite delight.

Slipping past the rocky cleft,
Streams of silver, deftly left.
Sprightly rush, a twinkling gleam,
Of the world, a liquid dream.

Spirits splashing, pure and bright,
Weaving tales in morning light.
Journey through the mossy bend,
Onward flow, with joy no end.

Merry Murmurs

Under the whispering stars,
Laughter lights the night.
Softly, joy flutters,
In twinkling, gentle flight.

Moonbeams dancing bright,
Casting silvery glow.
Heartbeats quicken pace,
In the merry flow.

Dreams drift through air,
Hopes shine within eyes.
Murmurs form a chorus,
Beneath celestial skies.

Hands held, voices low,
Smiles shared, warm embrace.
Happiness finds a home,
In this quiet, cherished place.

Night's soft serenade,
Melodies so sweet.
Merry murmurs weave,
In the world beneath our feet.

Forest Frolic

Verdant canopies high,
Whisper secrets old.
Dappled light cascades,
Green and gold enfold.

Footsteps soft on moss,
Nature's carpet laid.
Birdsong breaks the hush,
Harmonious parade.

Leaves dance with the wind,
Branches share their grace.
Shadows play and sway,
In this serene space.

Streams sing playful tunes,
Rocks laugh in delight.
Life bursts from every nook,
In morning, noon, and night.

Forest's heart beats strong,
Echoes ancient lore.
Frolic in its embrace,
Discover evermore.

Stream Songs

Beneath the azure sky,
Rivers weave their tale.
Waters hum their song,
Through valley, hill, and dale.

Pebbles click in rhythm,
Current's joy displayed.
Whispers of the wild,
In liquid notes, conveyed.

Frogs call out the chorus,
Fish weave melodies.
Symphony arises,
Amid the rustling trees.

Eddies spin a story,
Bubbles laugh and leap.
Nature's choir gathered,
In harmony so deep.

Stream songs gently lull,
Hearts to peace and dream.
Let the waters guide,
On this melodious stream.

Meander Merriment

Paths wind through the vale,
Journeys intertwined.
Every twist and turn,
New delights to find.

Flowers greet with smiles,
Grass whispers sweet luck.
Butterflies dance light,
In the golden cluck.

Sunlight's playful rays,
Skip from leaf to leaf.
Nature's jesters jest,
In joy without grief.

Steps lead to laughter,
Voices filled with cheer.
Meander through merriment,
All you hold dear.

Life's a winding road,
Moments to be spent.
Find bliss in each curve,
Pure and innocent.

Riparian Revels

Beneath the willows, whispers fly,
Over ripples, time drifts by.
Cedars hum a soft refrain,
Nature's chorus greets the rain.

Emerald meadows stretch afar,
Mirrored moons in waters are.
Herons glide on gentle streams,
Riparian realm of waking dreams.

Dew-kissed mornings, fresh and bright,
Songs of crickets fill the night.
Each leaf dances to the tune,
Echoes fade beneath the moon.

In this haven, wild and free,
Every ripple holds a key.
To the secrets, tales untold,
Riparian dreams of ages old.

Sunlit Soiree

Golden rays of summer's day,
Children's laughter guiding way.
Field of flowers, colors sprung,
Morning melodies are sung.

Butterflies on gossamer wings,
Nature's concert softly rings.
Shade of oak, a resting place,
Sunbeams kiss each eager face.

Birds on high in azure sky,
Clouds like whispers float on by.
Petals open, greeting light,
Day transforms from dawn to night.

Joyful moments in the breeze,
Time stands still among the trees.
Blessed warmth of solar play,
In the magic of this day.

Sebaceous Symphony

In the night, a gleaming hue,
Stars above, a wondrous view.
Flows of silver, silent streams,
Luminous, the world redeems.

Oils of midnight, shadows sway,
Soft and silky, dark ballet.
Moonlit whispers, tales confide,
Dreams are where the wonders hide.

Twilight oaths in velvet's care,
Secret murmurs fill the air.
Ebony and silver glide,
Symphony of night complied.

Each dark droplet, purest art,
From creation, worlds depart.
In the silence, beauty's key,
Sebaceous night, eternity.

Mirthful Mergers

Hands and hearts in joyful union,
Echoes of a grand communion.
Smiles exchanged like secret songs,
Where happiness so rightly belongs.

Bounding steps in dance and cheer,
Friendship's laughter, ringing clear.
Life's a waltz of fates entwined,
With each partner sweetly kind.

Shared adventures, stories spun,
Beneath the same resplendent sun.
Moments stitched with threads of gold,
In each other, futures bold.

Harmonized in joy and plight,
Souls together, burning bright.
Boundless joy, love converges,
Life's pure bliss in mirthful mergers.

Aquatic Antics

Bubbles rise in playful glee,
Under waves, a world set free,
Fins and tails in dance delight,
Moonlit waters come alive at night.

Crabs in cadence tap their claws,
Fish dart through with no pause,
Seahorses sway in coral care,
Currents whisper secrets rare.

Starfish gleam in tideline hues,
Anemones with vibrant views,
Octopus in inked disguise,
Mysteries hidden in their eyes.

Jellyfish float with ghostly grace,
Dolphins carve a joyful trace,
Turtle timeless, glides so deep,
Ocean's cradle, where dreams sleep.

Whales sing in deep refrain,
Rhythms cast on boundless main,
Watery world, a serene trance,
Aquatic antics in nature's dance.

Rivers Unfold

Winding path through valley green,
Whispers low, a peaceful scene,
Rivers tell of ages past,
In their ripples shadows cast.

Stones beneath, smoothed by time,
Echoes of a silent rhyme,
Canyons carved by gentle streams,
Flow eternal like our dreams.

Forests bow to liquid trails,
Softly hum the traveler's tales,
Bridges arch with graceful hands,
Linking hearts across the lands.

Silver shimmer in the sun,
Journey's end and yet begun,
Life abundant at each turn,
Lessons of the river learn.

Mighty rivers, mighty tales,
In your depths, the secret sails,
Nature's map, in waters told,
Dreams forever rivers unfold.

Streams of Delight

Softly winding through the glen,
Hidden paths from now and then,
Crickets' serenade at night,
Streams are flowing, pure delight.

Pebbles dance beneath the flow,
Where the mint and daisies grow,
Sunbeams kiss the surface slight,
Rippling gems in morning light.

Murmur sweet, a soothing call,
Water's edge where pine trees tall,
Nature's song in notes so bright,
Streams are whispers of the light.

Dappled shade and sleepy blooms,
Onyx pools where silence looms,
Dragonflies in aerial flight,
Streams of wonder spark delight.

Through the hills and valleys dream,
Life meanders like a stream,
Finding peace in shadows slight,
Walking paths of pure delight.

Trickle and Purr

Mountain tops to meadows green,
Tiny trickles start unseen,
Gather strength in gentle blur,
Streams that ripple, trickle, purr.

Through the moss and fern they weave,
Nature's secrets they conceive,
Bringing life to thirsty roots,
Softly sung in brook's pursuits.

Waterfalls descend with might,
Morning mist in dawn's first light,
Whispers float on breezes stir,
Magic in the trickle, purr.

Pebbled paths they carve anew,
Every turn a passage through,
Harmony in liquid blur,
Notes of nature, trickle, purr.

Life's own journey in a stream,
Quietly they build the dream,
Eternal flow where dreams occur,
Ever flowing, trickle, purr.

Submerged Smiles

In depths where shadows softly sway,
Whispers of the ocean play.
Joyful ripples kiss the night,
Submerged smiles in moon's light.

Coral castles guard secrets deep,
Wave's embrace where treasures sleep.
Visions clear in water's gaze,
Submerged smiles in mystic haze.

Schools of fish in silver dance,
Breathless moments caught by chance.
Silent laughter with each mile,
Submerged smiles make hearts compile.

Bubble trails to surface climb,
Echoes of an ocean rhyme.
Mermaid dreams and sand's fine pile,
Submerged smiles in tranquil isle.

Splash and Sparkle

Morning sun on waters bright,
Diamonds dance in pure delight.
Liquid laughter, pure and free,
Splash and sparkle, wild and glee.

Rainbow shards in droplets spin,
Nature's jewels on skin and fin.
Every splash a burst of cheer,
Splash and sparkle, drawing near.

Frolicking in azure waves,
Playful spirits summer saves.
Every dive and twirl so bold,
Splash and sparkle, tales unfold.

Golden rays in warm embrace,
Nature's kiss on every face.
Moments fleeting, yet they stay,
Splash and sparkle, light the day.

Sprightly Splash

Lazy rivers twist and curl,
Nature's secrets they unfurl.
Whispers of a sprightly splash,
In the sunlight, moments flash.

Dragonflies on wings of blue,
Dipping low in morning dew.
Ripples weave a gentle tale,
Sprightly splash and breezes pale.

Leaping fish and skimming stones,
Songs of summer, nature's tones.
Carefree in a timeless dash,
Serenade of sprightly splash.

Water's laughter, pure and bright,
Chasing through the waning light.
Joy in every golden beam,
Sprightly splash, a waking dream.

Euphoric Eddies

Spinning in a dance so grand,
Waters carve and shape the land.
Endless whirl in liquid form,
Euphoric eddies in the storm.

Catching sunlight as they turn,
Glowing embers in the churn.
Rhythms in the churning foam,
Euphoric eddies call us home.

Mystic spirals touch the soul,
Moving hearts where waters roll.
Life's ballet in fluid sweep,
Euphoric eddies, secrets keep.

Voices in the river's song,
Guiding us and moving strong.
In their depths, the world they show,
Euphoric eddies, onward flow.

Dancing with Driftwood

On the shore, where waves do crest,
We dance in twilight's fleeting boon,
Driftwood partners in the west,
Beneath a silver slivered moon.

Footprints trace a fleeting tale,
By night, overlooked by eyes,
Whispers softly on the gale,
As starlight sparkles, ever wise.

Thalassic murmurs call the night,
A symphony of sea and time,
Echoes crest, their sound takes flight,
In rhythm, pure, and sublime.

Silhouettes in moonlit trance,
Nature's waltz so finely tuned,
The ocean bids us all to dance,
With driftwood, endlessly attuned.

Horizon's hues begin to glow,
A dawn reborn, our dance conclude,
In memories where breezes blow,
We're dancing with the driftwood, renewed.

Fancy of the Falls

Glistening droplets in descent,
A dance of light and liquid grace,
Nature's song, so eloquent,
Falls cascade with tender pace.

Rainbows weave through misty veil,
Colors arch in sheer delight,
The waterfall's enchanting tale,
Unfolds beneath the morning light.

Each cascade a gentle prayer,
To earth and sky, the falls do sing,
In melodies that drift through air,
Nature's symphony in spring.

Emerald moss and ferny glade,
Embrace the waters' silky flow,
Whispered secrets, softly bade,
Where myths and ancient echoes go.

A place where dreams and waters meet,
In nature's chamber, vast and wide,
The fancy of the falls complete,
A timeless dance we'll not deride.

Streamside Serenade

Beneath the canopies so green,
A melody of crystal clear,
Streams hum softly, so serene,
Nature's music, we draw near.

Pebbles paint the glassy bed,
In patterns only waters know,
Each note by their caress is fed,
As downstream silvery currents flow.

Birdsong joins the soft refrain,
A symphony of life unfurls,
In hues of dawn, the light's domain,
A dance of shadows, eddies swirls.

The streamside breeze in whispers low,
Carries tales of times unlived,
With every ripple, every flow,
A gentle song by earth is given.

In this tranquil, sacred place,
Where nature's chorus never fades,
We find our hearts in its embrace,
And cherish the streamside serenades.

Twilight Tumblers

In twilight's hush, where shadows play,
The tumblers come to life anew,
Soft twilight hues at end of day,
Dappled light in softest blue.

On fields where fireflies take flight,
They dance in spirals, wild and free,
A ballet in the falling night,
Unseen by all but moon and tree.

Stars awake to watch the show,
With twinkles bright in darkened sky,
The tumblers leap, they ebb, they flow,
In graceful arcs as time drifts by.

They twirl on breezes, light as dreams,
Silent whispers through the air,
In twilight's canvas, streaked in creams,
Their essence moving everywhere.

When dawn's first light begins to creep,
The tumblers fade with morning's hue,
While memories in hearts we keep,
Of twilight's dance, forever true.

Harmonious Hucklebucks

In fields of green where daisies bloom,
The Hucklebucks in gentle swoon,
They dance to tunes of nature's choir,
Their hearts alight with pure desire.

Underneath the sky's embrace,
Joyful steps, they set the pace,
Rhythms blend in evening's hush,
Harmony in every crush.

Twilight whispers secrets low,
In their eyes, a vibrant glow,
Hucklebucks in moon's soft beam,
Living dreams within a dream.

Each twirl writes a timeless song,
With movements right, both swift and strong,
Their laughter floats among the leaves,
On nights where magic never leaves.

Together, hand in hand they sway,
In meadows where they love to play,
United by the bond they share,
In dances free of any care.

Surface Serenades

Gentle waves on silver seas,
Whispering with tongues of breeze,
Sing to stars in twilight's shade,
Nature's sweet, serene parade.

Luna's light upon the water,
Echoes songs from Earth's own daughter,
Sweeping tales of love, unknown,
In a world of salt and stone.

Boats drift on the tranquil tide,
To the music, they confide,
Waves caress in soft lament,
Melodies of time well spent.

Horizon hums to skies aglow,
With silent notes that subtly flow,
Sailors dream on gentle swells,
To the sound of ocean bells.

Each ripple plays a part so fine,
In the sea's eternal line,
Surface serenades in flight,
Beneath the canopy of night.

Bathers' Bliss

In waters warm, where sunbeams kiss,
Bathers find their deepest bliss,
Floating free on liquid gold,
In stories yet to be retold.

Ripples dance on crystal blue,
Where laughter mingles, bright and true,
Joy refracts in sparkling light,
Moments caught in pure delight.

Soft waves cradle dreams with care,
In this realm where hearts can dare,
To feel the gentle, soothing tide,
In quiet pools where love resides.

Whispers of the water's song,
Carry souls on journeys long,
To places where the heart's at ease,
In currents soft as autumn's breeze.

Bathers bask in calm retreat,
In liquid embrace, mild and sweet,
Their spirits lifted, light as air,
In the water's tender care.

Ebullient Edges

On cliffs where eagles dare to soar,
The edges call with zest and more,
Embracing winds with fervent cry,
To touch the vast, unending sky.

Atop the world where clouds convene,
A radiant, untamed serene,
Wildflowers dance in colors bright,
In ebullience of morning light.

Footprints trace a journey bold,
Stories of adventures told,
The horizon's beckoning allure,
Promises of dreams, unsure.

With every step, the heart expands,
To understand life's shifting sands,
Edges brimming with delight,
As dawn unveils her wings of light.

In this place where spirits sing,
Ebullience in everything,
Boundless joy that never ends,
On life's edges, hearts transcend.

Splendid Streams

In dappled light the waters gleam,
Whispered tales by banks so green.
Nature's song, a peaceful theme,
In splendid streams, a tranquil scene.

Pebbles dance beneath the flow,
Reflecting skies in azure glow.
Harmony in constant show,
Through splendid streams, the rivers go.

Echoes of the forest's cheer,
Ripples gentle, crystal clear.
Time stands still, the mind sincere,
In splendid streams devoid of fear.

Journey far where waters wind,
Mysteries of life to find.
Serenades of the brook unwind,
In splendid streams, hearts and minds.

Life breathes through this quiet grace,
Flowing with a tender pace.
Moments here we can't replace,
In splendid streams, a pure embrace.

Whisker Waltzes

In moonlit nights where shadows play,
Silent steps, a dance display.
Softly through the grass they stray,
In whisker waltzes, night meets day.

Graceful moves in secret lanes,
Echoes of their soft refrains.
Feline whispers, breaking chains,
Through whisker waltzes, joy remains.

Silken fur in twilight's gleam,
Eyes that hold a thousand dreams.
Purring softly like a stream,
In whisker waltzes, peace redeems.

Through the quiet, tails entwine,
Hearts beat softly, all align.
Harmony in night's design,
In whisker waltzes, souls incline.

Silent nights yet full of song,
Breathing life the whole night long.
Mystic rhythms pure and strong,
In whisker waltzes, we belong.

Flowing Frolics

Life awakens with a splash,
Playful currents, boulders dash.
Joy in every cheerful crash,
In flowing frolics, waters flash.

Sunlight dances on each crest,
waves engaged in merry jest.
Nature's laughter, never stressed,
Through flowing frolics, hearts are blessed.

Mossy banks with secrets told,
Streams of silver, streams of gold.
Mysteries of life unfold,
In flowing frolics, ages old.

Leaves caught in a whirlpool's song,
Spirits where they truly belong.
Soothing winds that drift along,
In flowing frolics, pure and strong.

Moments of unending cheer,
Waterways that crystal clear.
Happiness in forms sincere,
In flowing frolics, we draw near.

River Radiance

Glimmering beneath the sun,
River's journey just begun.
Magic in each drop begun,
In river radiance, life's fun.

Reflections of the sky above,
Twilight painted, moments, love.
Flowing with the stars thereof,
In river radiance, pushed and shoved.

Waves embrace, a tender greet,
Melodies where waters meet.
Carried by a rhythmic beat,
Through river radiance, life's sweet.

Banks adorned with verdant grace,
Nature's bounty we embrace.
Every ripple leaves a trace,
In river radiance, time's space.

Morning dew and evening glow,
Stories told in gentle flow.
Wonder in each ebb and tow,
In river radiance, we grow.

Brookside Bliss

A whispering stream, through meadows wide,
Crickets chirp, and shadows glide,
The water's song, a lullaby,
Beneath the cerulean sky.

Pebbles kissed by tender waves,
Echo tales of hidden caves,
Sunlight dances on the crest,
Nature's harmony at its best.

Dragonflies with wings so bright,
Hover o'er in gleeful flight,
They twirl and dip, in liquid air,
In this tranquil, sunlit lair.

Branches bow to greet the flow,
Where moss and fern in stillness grow,
A symphony in green and blue,
Pure serenity, through and through.

The brookside murmurs soft and clear,
A melody for hearts to hear,
In this nook, away from strife,
Find the gentle pulse of life.

Eddy Euphoria

In a world where eddies twirl,
Water's dance, a glassy swirl,
Rippling circles, spreading wide,
Joy in motion, side by side.

Gleaming shards of liquid light,
Reflections mirroring delight,
Froth and bubble, playful cheer,
Nature's laughter ringing here.

Smooth stones polished, round and bright,
Turn and tumble in their flight,
Synopsis of the water's way,
Endless journey, night and day.

Leaves adrift, a gentle ride,
Eddy's spin is nature's glide,
A tranquil maze, a liquid spin,
Harmony, where flow begins.

Stars above, the night's caress,
Mirrored in the water's press,
Eddies whisper tales unseen,
In their murmurs, pure serene.

Currents of Cheer

Currents weave a joyful thread,
In the river's ample bed,
Shimmering paths, a dance of light,
Canvas painted day and night.

Thrill of rushes, waters swift,
Every turn a lively gift,
Gleeful splashes, nature's grace,
Celebrate at every pace.

Fish dart quick in sparkling streams,
Chasing shadows, chasing dreams,
Playful currents guide their race,
In this boundless, bright embrace.

Branches dipped in water's sway,
Wave and beckon night and day,
Mysteries in the river's flow,
Endless wonder as they go.

Currents hum a gentle tune,
Underneath the watchful moon,
In their melody, so clear,
Lie the world's sweet notes of cheer.

Surges of Smiles

Upon the shore, the robins sing,
Announcing joyous everything,
The tides respond in happy sways,
Ushering in these sunny days.

Each wave that crashes, meets the sand,
Leaves behind a sparkling brand,
Footprints fade, replaced by glee,
In the rhythm of the sea.

Dolphins leap in arcs so high,
Tracing smiles in the sky,
Their playful surge, a sheer delight,
A testament to ocean might.

Golden rays on blue expanse,
Nature's own enchanting dance,
Surges bring a peace profound,
In their ceaseless, soothing sound.

Beneath the waves, where silence reals,
A world of wonder softly feels,
In the depths, and on the shores,
Surges sing and hearts explore.

Flowing Folly

In forests deep where shadows dance,
Rivers twirl in rhythmic trance,
Flowing freely, wild and keen,
Nature's folly, bright and green.

Whispers carried on the breeze,
Songs of laughter through the trees,
Skipping stones and giggling streams,
Life a tapestry of dreams.

Sunlight glistens on the waves,
Sparkling paths to hidden caves,
Every turn a new surprise,
Morning's glow meets evening skies.

Majestic waters write their lore,
Tales of joy and so much more,
In the heart of nature's spin,
Life and love and journeys begin.

Echoes of a world so free,
Nature's dance in harmony,
Flowing folly, cherish thee,
In the wild, our souls agree.

Ecstatic Estuaries

Where land meets sea in soft embrace,
Estuaries find their sacred place,
Tides that whisper, waves that gleam,
A confluence of hopes unseen.

Mangroves dance with roots so deep,
In waters where the brackish sleep,
Songs of life in every splash,
Dreams in tides that ebb and dash.

Nature's pulse in silent beat,
Estuaries where earth and sea meet,
Splashing blue, a tranquil blend,
Journeys start and journeys end.

Birds above with wings spread wide,
Soaring high where waters guide,
In the delta's warm caress,
Find a home of endless bless.

Ecstatic joy in each spring tide,
Nature's spirit amplified,
In these waters life restored,
Harmony forever more.

Ripples in the Stream

Gentle streams in twilight's grace,
Ripples form a soft embrace,
Liquid mirrors catch the sky,
Reflections where our dreams lie.

Pebbles tossed in playful throw,
Circles widening, gracefully flow,
Moments shared in silent gleam,
Whispers of a cherished dream.

Clouds drift by in painted hues,
Ripples dance, a tranquil muse,
Waters weave their tender song,
In the stillness we belong.

Nature's breath in ripples passed,
Moments fleeting, never last,
Yet their beauty, gentle beam,
Lives forever in the stream.

Peace in every ripple's spread,
Silent echoes in our stead,
Touched by waters' pure delight,
Day turns softly into night.

Aquatic Playfulness

Dancing waters, playful spree,
Life beneath in jubilee,
Splash and sing in sunlight's glow,
Aquatic play fills the flow.

Fish that dart in gleeful chase,
Weaving tales in lively grace,
Bubbles rise in joyful cheer,
Echoes of a world so clear.

Children laugh on riverbanks,
Feet submerged, they give their thanks,
Nature's playground, wild and free,
Bonding in its purity.

Sunset paints the water's edge,
Golden hues and glistening pledge,
Every drop a world entire,
A symphony, a choir.

Moments in the sunlit streams,
Closer to our wildest dreams,
Aquatic mirth, a joyous quest,
With nature's play, we are blessed.

Synchronized Swims

In liquid depths, they twist and turn,
With graceful arcs, they softly churn.
Under water's cool embrace,
A ballet unfolds, a delicate trace.

Bright fins flash, a rhythmic beat,
Patterns woven where currents meet.
In unison, they dive and rise,
A dance of beauty beneath the skies.

Echoes sound in the watery dome,
As fish find their synchronized home.
In perfect sync, they navigate,
In the serene, they celebrate.

Ripples spread with silent grace,
Marking paths in this aquatic space.
With each move, a tale is spun,
Of unity in the ocean's run.

Synchronized swims, nature's art,
A symphony where rhythms start.
Under waves, they move as one,
In the dance beneath the sun.

Riverside Rhapsody

By the banks where willows weep,
The river sings a song so deep.
Flowing notes of water's charm,
In nature's choir, there's no alarm.

Pebbles hum as currents kiss,
Creating music, a gentle bliss.
Birds join in with trills so sweet,
At the riverside, all worlds meet.

Dragonflies with wings of lace,
Hover in this tranquil space.
Reflections of the azure sky,
On water's surface, dreams lie.

Whispers of the evening breeze,
Rustle through the leafy trees.
Harmony in every sound,
In the rhapsody, peace is found.

Riverside rhapsody at play,
A symphony at the end of day.
Nature's melody, pure and free,
A timeless, flowing, symphony.

Glimmering Glides

Glimmers dance on water's face,
A sparkling ballet of light's embrace.
Sunbeams ripple on the tide,
In shimmering glides, they softly hide.

Silver fish weave through the glow,
Glimpses of beauty, they bestow.
Waves whisper secrets, stories told,
In liquid gold, the tales unfold.

Morning dew meets ocean's kiss,
Creating moments of pure bliss.
Reflections paint a moving art,
Of glimmering glides, a world apart.

Seagulls trace the sky's bright line,
Their shadows merge with the brine.
In harmony, they glide so fair,
In this light-kissed, breezy air.

As night descends, stars align,
Mingling with the ocean's shine.
Glimmering glides, a wondrous scene,
Where sea and light in dance convene.

Beneath the Surface

Beneath the surface, a hidden land,
Where silent waves touch the sand.
Mysteries whisper in the deep,
Secrets that the ocean keeps.

Coral castles, vibrant hues,
In this realm of countless clues.
Fish dart through a maze of night,
In phosphorescent, gentle light.

Anemones sway in ocean's breath,
In this world untouched by death.
Tides that pull and softly call,
Reveal the wonder of it all.

Mermaid legends, old and wise,
Live beneath the surface skies.
Songs of ancient seas they sing,
In the language of the spring.

Diving deep, one glimpse we see,
Of the ocean's mystery.
Beneath the waves, life's symphony,
Plays its tune, wild and free.

Bubbling Beneath

A world below the mirrored sheen,
Where sunlight dapples, soft, serene.
In depths where shadows seldom play,
Life's hidden dance, both night and day.

Silent whispers, currents glide,
Along the kelp, where creatures hide.
Colors burst in secret thrall,
A realm where mysteries call.

Rocks encrusted, stories old,
Of ancient tides and ships foretold.
Bubbles rise with secrets cast,
From seabed's grip to surface fast.

Schooling fish like silver beams,
Weave through waters, chasing dreams.
In the quiet, worlds collide,
In the deep, where wonders bide.

Seaweed's sway like dancer's steps,
A ballet where the ocean wept.
Bubbling beneath, the silence sings,
Of ocean's depths and untold things.

Ecstatic Eddies

Swirling pools of mirth and glee,
Where streams converge in harmony.
Nestled in the river's bend,
Where laughter's currents never end.

Pebbles tumble, stories told,
Of waters young and journeys bold.
Each twist and turn, a dance in kind,
Eddies weave what fate designed.

Mirthful bubbles rise and spin,
A liquid waltz that draws you in.
With grace, they twirl in joyful spree,
A water laugh, an eddy's plea.

Ripples radiate with cheer,
Eddies whisper in your ear.
Come join our dance, they softly call,
In the stream where spirits fall.

Circles form, then drift apart,
A liquid ballet from the heart.
Ecstatic eddies, ever true,
In each embrace, the world anew.

Otter's Odyssey

Through rivers wide and oceans blue,
An otter's quest, a journey true.
With whiskers keen and fur so sleek,
He prowls the waters, brave and meek.

Clams to crack and fish to gleam,
Each day unfolds a brand new dream.
In every tide and every crest,
An odyssey, a life's bequest.

Through forests dense where rivers wind,
In gentle streams, his path aligned.
A journey vast, a tale to tell,
In every brook and hidden dell.

Playful dives and somersaults,
Through wave and tide, where water vaults.
An otter's world, so full, so free,
In liquid realms of mystery.

From dawn till dusk, his journey flows,
Where water whispers, he follows.
An odyssey of life and cheer,
An otter's path, both far and near.

Water Whiskers

Soft whiskers trace the water's edge,
Where river meets the grassy ledge.
In twilight's glow, their dance begins,
A touch so light, like gentle winds.

Whiskers dip and senses flare,
In liquid dusk, with utmost care.
They chart the depths, the currents wild,
Each ripple felt, like a child.

Tiny tremors, whispers swift,
Through murky depths, they deftly sift.
Under moon's watch, their journey starts,
With whispers light, the whiskers' arts.

Streamside grasses, moonlit beams,
Reflecting nature's quiet dreams.
Water whiskers, tender bright,
Exploring worlds in silent flight.

In waters deep and shadows vast,
Their whispers weave a spell that's cast.
Through fluid realms, with grace they whisk,
In nature's hand, their magic brisk.

Furry Frolics

In meadows green they leap with glee,
Soft fur dancing, wild and free.
Chasing shadows, tails held high,
Underneath the boundless sky.

Little paws in playful stride,
Through the bushes, side by side.
Cheerful barks and joyous mews,
Soft whispers in the morning dew.

Nimble feet on dewy grass,
Moments in the sunlight pass.
Whiskers twitch in morning light,
Happy hearts take to flight.

Whirling winds of furry fun,
Until the setting of the sun.
Savoring the day's delight,
Dreams begin with coming night.

In their sleep, they prance anew,
Mystic lands where blossoms grew.
Roaming realms of verdant bliss,
Furry frolics end with this.

Splashing Serenades

Rippling waves sing songs so pure,
Against the shore, they call demure.
Casting droplets in the air,
Moments captured, free from care.

Feet in water, cool and bright,
Laughter dances in the light.
Sparkling melodies abound,
Nature's harmony profound.

Tides in whispers, secrets share,
Underneath the sun's warm glare.
Echoes of the ocean's song,
Joyful hums where we belong.

Gentle splashes, rhythms blend,
Timeless tunes that never end.
Water's voice, a symphony,
Singing nature's jubilee.

Softly now, the day does fade,
Moonbeams lend their tender shade.
Serenades of splashing cheer,
Linger in our hearts so near.

River Romp

Through the valley's verdant spread,
Winding waters gently thread.
Sunlight glints on ripples clear,
River's song, a tune so dear.

Children laugh and pebbles skip,
Over stones where minnows slip.
Grassy banks with flowers crowned,
Nature's chorus all around.

Boats that drift and currents glide,
In the river's easy tide.
Whispers of the water flow,
Secrets only rivers know.

Branches dip in liquid trails,
Winds bring stories, ancient tales.
Every bend and silent nook,
Writes a page within its book.

When the twilight's shadows play,
Turn to gold the end of day.
River romps forever stay,
In our hearts, they hold their sway.

Chasing Sunbeams

Morning mist in meadow's grasp,
Golden rays they seek and clasp.
Sunbeams dance in waking hours,
Touching petals, kissing flowers.

Children's laughter fills the air,
Round and round they run with care.
Chasing beams of vibrant light,
Through the day and into night.

Fields of green and sky so blue,
Every hue a dazzling view.
Running free with hearts aglow,
Music in their every show.

Through the woods and over hills,
Mystic land where silence thrills.
Sunbeams play their hide-and-seek,
Magic moments, bright and sleek.

When the day begins to fade,
Sunset colors softly played.
Memories of beams once chased,
In their dreams so gently traced.

Furry Frolic

In meadows wide, where tall grass sways,
With paws so light and spirits high,
A dance begins beneath the rays.
Beneath the bright and open sky.

Through fields of blooms, they bound and leap,
Their fur a blur of joyous haze,
With every step, a secret keep,
Of nature's gentle, playful ways.

The morning dew on whiskers' tips,
Reflects the light of dawn's embrace,
As laughter springs from tiny lips,
In this enchanted, wild space.

They chase the breeze and butterflies,
Among the trees, through golden glens,
Beneath the watch of azure skies,
Where innocence and freedom blend.

With tails a-flick and eyes alight,
Their world a wondrous, living dream,
In furry frolics, hearts take flight,
For love and life are their grand scheme.

Waterside Whimsy

Beside the brook, where willows weep,
The water whispers tales of lore,
In gentle murmurs, vows to keep,
It sings the songs of yesteryore.

The dragonflies on silver wings,
And reeds that dance in soft ballet,
Compose a tune that nature brings,
A symphony at break of day.

The lilies float like purest pearls,
And frogs in chorus croak their tune,
While ripples cast their gentle swirls,
Beneath the smiling face of moon.

In shadows cast by ancient trees,
The secrets of the deep unfold,
A testament to timeless seas,
With stories waiting to be told.

So come and sit by waterside,
Let whimsy wash your cares away,
Embrace the magic as it glides,
In nature's tender, warm caress.

Currents of Cheer

The river flows with vibrant grace,
It carries whispers from afar,
In every twist, a joyful trace,
Beneath the gaze of sun and star.

The laughter of the waters bright,
Reflects in eyes that wander near,
A constant stream of pure delight,
Embracing moments without fear.

From mountain peaks through valleys green,
It journeys onward, ever clear,
A ribbon in the nature's scene,
A source of endless, boundless cheer.

With every bend and playful splash,
It touches hearts in soft embrace,
Unfolding life in bright-eyed flash,
A testament to nature's grace.

So follow where the currents lead,
And find the cheer that waters bring,
With every step, fulfill the need,
To dance along and softly sing.

Dappled Delight

Beneath the leaves where sunbeams play,
With shadows dancing soft and light,
In forests deep, where spirits stay,
Resides a world of sheer delight.

The woodland floor, a tapestry,
Of mossy greens and earthy browns,
Invites the wandering souls like thee,
To lose themselves beyond the towns.

Birdsong echoes through the boughs,
A chorus sweet with morning dew,
And on the breeze, each note bestows,
A sense of wonder pure and true.

The dappled light, a painter's brush,
Creates a shifting, magic scene,
Where time slows down, and moments hush,
To bask in beauty so serene.

Step lightly through this sacred space,
Let nature be your guiding light,
In every leaf and tender trace,
Discover earth's pure, dappled delight.

Rippling Rhythms

The river sings a lullaby,
Underneath the star-streaked sky.
Whispers of a distant shore,
Echoes dance forevermore.

Moonbeams kiss the water's face,
In a slow, enchanting grace.
Ripples weave a melody,
Waves of time, sweet reverie.

Oars that dip in silent night,
Shadows waltz within the light.
Flowing dreams in gentle sway,
Guide the hearts that drift away.

Banks of memories trace the flow,
Years and years of ebb and glow.
Silent songs of old refrain,
Whisper 'til we're home again.

In the hush of twilight's gleam,
Nature hums a timeless theme.
Rippling rhythms sing so clear,
Melodies for hearts to hear.

Echoes of Elation

In the valley, joy resounds,
Laughter in the hills abounds.
Echoes carry far and near,
Songs of love for all to hear.

Morning's light and evening's hue,
Paint the skies with shades anew.
Whispers of the day gone by,
Scatter stardust in the sky.

Voices rise in sweet duet,
Every joy and each regret.
Mountains hold the tales we tell,
Echoed dreams in nature's spell.

Wind that carries notes so high,
Through the clouds, they softly fly.
Harmony in every breeze,
Serenade the rustling trees.

In this place where echoes start,
Feel the rhythm, every part.
Jubilance and pure delight,
Sing through shadows of the night.

Bankside Banter

By the river's playful grin,
Stories of old friends begin.
Laughter dances with the breeze,
Mirth beneath the willow trees.

Skipping stones and tales anew,
Children's chatter, skies of blue.
Echoes of a distant past,
Present moments never last.

Whispers of the leaves in spring,
Joy in every song they sing.
Life that flows in merry ways,
Bankside banter fills the days.

Footsteps mark the winding trail,
Nature joins in the tale.
Smiling faces, hearts set free,
In this dance of liberty.

River's edge, a sacred space,
Friendship blooms in every place.
Banter by the water's side,
Memories in currents ride.

Waterside Whimsy

Bubbles rise and laughter spills,
Over pebbles, down the hills.
Nature's playground, pure and bright,
Daylight turns to starry night.

Waters hum a cheerful tune,
Underneath the silver moon.
Frogs that croak and crickets sing,
Celebrate the joys of spring.

Children race along the shore,
Every step, a quest for more.
Skipping ropes and catching dreams,
Wading through the sunlit streams.

Fairy tales in water's flow,
Secrets only rivers know.
Whispers of the past they hold,
Stories waiting to be told.

Gentle ripples, lost in play,
Lead the mind where fantasies sway.
In the splash of whimsy's might,
Every heart finds pure delight.

Splash Dance

In the moonlight, rivers gleam,
Water's waltz, a silent dream.
Whirls and twirls, a gentle trance,
Nature's own, a splash dance.

Murmurs soft, the night does hum,
Ripples play, where currents drum.
Stars reflect in water's glance,
All partake in splash dance.

Glowing orbs in deer-eye view,
Critters join the river's cue.
Frogs and fish with fate enhance,
Pure delight, this splash dance.

Rays of dawn, the edge of light,
Breaking through the veil of night.
Still they move in happenstance,
Eternal, this splash dance.

Echoes whisper down the stream,
Life together, forest team.
Bound by waves, they all advance,
Partners in this splash dance.

Bankside Ballet

By the edge where waters sway,
Graceful reeds in soft display.
With each gust, they gently sway,
Dancing bankside ballet.

Feathered wings cut through the air,
Egrets float without a care.
In the dawn, a new bouquet,
Infinite bankside ballet.

Lilies bloom as frogs align,
Leaping in a perfect line.
Nature's stage, they share convey,
Harmonious bankside ballet.

Dragonflies in hues so bright,
Flit and twirl in morning light.
Petals part, they find their way,
Twisting bankside ballet.

Evening's glow now fades to night,
Still they move in twilight's sight.
Moonlit waves, a soft relay,
Timeless bankside ballet.

Bubbly Bliss

Tiny bubbles rise and gleam,
Water's whispers in a dream.
Playful orbs of purest kiss,
Life's delight in bubbly bliss.

Silver drops on petals rest,
Morning's dew in nature's nest.
Sunlight sparkles, none dismiss,
Moments wrapped in bubbly bliss.

Streams of laughter, joy's own call,
Glistening waves, serene and small.
Echoes carry warmth's caress,
Bound in love and bubbly bliss.

Under skies of endless blue,
Children's smiles, fresh as dew.
Simple joys no soul can miss,
Magic found in bubbly bliss.

Calm and peace in bubbles show,
Gentle hums that softly grow.
Heartfelt whispers, nature's kiss,
Eternal bond in bubbly bliss.

Ripple Romp

Skipping stones on liquid glass,
Breaking peace where ripples pass.
Circles widen, shadows chomp,
Joyous play, a ripple romp.

Skipping feet on water's edge,
Dancing past the willow's hedge.
Echoes, whispers, jump and clomp,
Echo the bliss of ripple romp.

Sunlit streams, a golden thread,
Through the currents swiftly spread.
Nature's rhythm, hop and stomp,
Infinite fun of ripple romp.

Mossy banks where crickets sing,
Joyous children, laughs they bring.
Splash and dash to nature's pomp,
Bound by love in ripple romp.

Daylight fades, but not the glee,
Water's dance in twilight's sea.
Night ensures the dreams will romp,
Endless tales in ripple romp.

Innocence of the River

Where waters gently weave and wend,
A secret tale they do defend.
Reflections dance upon the crest,
Of nature's secrets, river-blessed.

Beneath the willow's shaded sigh,
Whispers trace the azure sky.
The song of water, pure and sweet,
Where earth and heaven softly meet.

Pebbles kissed by gentle waves,
Innocence in hidden caves.
Fish darting like silver beams,
Rivers holding ancient dreams.

Wildflowers bloom along the edge,
A tender life in whisper's pledge.
Ripples, laughter, stories told,
In river's heart, the young hold gold.

Evening falls with soft embrace,
Stars reflected in water's face.
Rustling leaves in twilight's hymns,
River's lullaby softly dims.

Flowing Fables

Tales untold in waters clear,
Ancient stories whispered near.
Flowing fables, wisdom's thread,
In the current's quiet spread.

Dragonflies on mirrored glass,
Past and present, shadows cast.
Each ripple births a chapter new,
In flowing fables, myths accrue.

Rivers carve the legends old,
Waves of wonder, dreams unfold.
Eagle's flight and cedar's tale,
Nature's lore on water's trail.

Murmurs of the elder trees,
Float upon the summer breeze.
Songs inscribed in liquid line,
Flowing fables intertwine.

In the dusk, the stories rest,
Sunset's glow upon their crest.
Fables flow in endless streams,
Rivers' hearts, the keepers' dreams.

Marshland Merriment

Upon the marsh, where cattails sway,
Joyful creatures spend their day.
Frogs in chorus, crickets sing,
Marshland's heart, a lively ring.

In the reeds, the herons stand,
Guardians of this jeweled land.
Turtles bask in sunny grace,
Nature's laughter, soft embrace.

Dragonflies with wings of light,
Dance through marshes, gentle flight.
Beavers' dams in wetlands wide,
Crafting homes with utmost pride.

Lily pads like emerald fleets,
Float where water softly meets.
Playful otters, sleek and swift,
Marshland's joy, a precious gift.

Twilight falls with hues of gold,
Marshland tales in whispers told.
Merriment in moonlight's glow,
Nature's joy in ebb and flow.

Whiskered Wonders

Beneath the starlit canopy,
Whiskered wonders roam so free.
Silent prowls on velvet paws,
Nature's hunters, without flaws.

Eyes aglow in moonlit night,
Silent shadows take their flight.
Mystery in every glance,
Whiskered wonders' nightly dance.

Through the forest, sleek and sly,
Echoes of their stealthy cry.
Ancient wisdom in their stride,
In shadow's realm, they confide.

Graceful movement, silent sweep,
Guardians of the dark they keep.
Mysterious and ever bold,
Tales of whiskered wonders told.

Morning light will chase the dark,
Yet they fade without a mark.
Whiskered wonders slip away,
Till night returns with soft array.

Streamside Laughter

By the babbling brook we roam,
Silver glimmers wet our toes.
Joyful echoes bind us close,
Nature's secrets now our home.

Sunlight dances, leaves cascade,
Under whispering canopy.
Laughter flows like streams of jade,
Boundless youth in melody.

Songs of birds ignite the morn,
Winds entwine in playful race.
Whispered dreams on breezes born,
Echoes filled with grace.

In each ripple, tales unfold,
Mirrors of the sky above.
Streamside laughter, pure as gold,
Nature's endless love.

Nimble Navigators

Amid the sky so wild and free,
Birds traverse the boundless air.
Feathers glint like stars at sea,
Horizon beckons without care.

Wings aflash, they rise and glide,
Minds attuned to nature's call.
Every gust their trusted guide,
In the vast skies, they enthrall.

Over mountains, past the streams,
Through the clouds, a swift ballet.
Guided by forgotten dreams,
Nimble navigators sway.

Their journeys carve the azure ink,
Geography of open flight.
Bound by wayward winds they link,
Day shall bow to night.

Nature's Ballet

At dawn's first light the act begins,
Curtains part as dewdrops gleam.
Every leaf and flower spins,
Nature dances in a dream.

Breath of morning sets the stage,
Whispers start the tender sway.
Actors twirl with unseen sage,
In Nature's grand ballet.

Petals stretch in steps so chore,
Sunbeams cast a golden ray.
Winds compose their joyous score,
Harmony in soft array.

As twilight falls, the dance remains,
Stars now don their silver crowns.
Hearts uplift in gentle strains,
Nature's ballet winding down.

Waves of Laughter

Ocean tides in rhythmic cheer,
Wave and wind in mirthful play.
Children's voices sharp and clear,
Blend with surf in bright array.

Sands entwine with salty spray,
Footprints mark a fleeting trail.
Gulls above in swooping fray,
Breeze unfurls the sailor's tale.

Steps align in time with waves,
Echoes of the laughter's crest.
In each splash, a memory saves,
Sunset paints the ocean's breast.

Every breaker brings a smile,
Joy cascades in foamy mirth.
Seaside laughter, free of guile,
Stories woven by the earth.

Subtle Splashes

In the quiet dawn's embrace,
Ripples weave a tender maze,
Water whispers, secrets blend,
Soft impressions without end.

Pebbles dance with muted grace,
In the liquid mirror's face,
Reflections shimmer, gently tease,
Harmonies with whispered ease.

Cool touch upon the weary skin,
Where such subtle splashes begin,
Nature's poem in liquid form,
In tranquil pools, safe and warm.

Leaves above a solemn guard,
Casting shade in still regard,
Sunlight filters soft as lace,
In the silent water's place.

Echoes of a gentle brush,
Quiet moments, no rush,
Subtle splashes, dreams align,
In the water, peace defined.

Murky Merriment

Beneath the tangled willow's sweep,
In the shadowed pond so deep,
Lies a world of hidden cheer,
Murky waters, laughter clear.

Amidst the reeds and mud they play,
Creatures of the dusk and day,
Darting swift through greenish haze,
In their secret, joyful ways.

Frogs on lilypads convene,
In their murky, muted sheen,
Merriment beneath the veil,
In their stories, we regale.

Whispers in the twilight blend,
Tales of joy that never end,
In the darkness, hearts alight,
Murky waters, pure delight.

Life unseen, yet full of song,
Nature's hidden, vibrant throng,
In the silence, life unfolds,
Murky merriment it holds.

Rill Romp

A streamlet winds through vale and hill,
With joyous romp and endless thrill,
It sings a song both bright and free,
A rill's adventure, wild and spree.

Pebbles churn beneath its flow,
As onward with a gleeful glow,
The rill romps through the lush and green,
A sparkling dart in nature's scene.

Bouncing over stones with glee,
In its playful, light decree,
It whispers secrets to the trees,
As it dances with the breeze.

Children's laughter blends in tune,
With the rill's enlivened croon,
Heartfelt echoes in its rush,
In the romp, a joyful hush.

Flowing freely, wild and bright,
In the day and through the night,
Rill's adventure never stops,
In the woodland, rill's free hops.

Swirling Smiles

In the brook where laughter gleams,
Swirls of joy in sunlit beams,
Water twinkles, heart beguiled,
In every turn, a swirling smile.

Rays of sunshine kiss the stream,
Silver ripples like a dream,
Dancing light and shadow play,
In the water's lively sway.

Minnows dart with gleeful flash,
Amidst the stones and whispers splash,
Swirling movements, gentle grace,
Smiles reflected in their trace.

Leaves descend in swirling dance,
Nature's tender, vivid trance,
Each a smile in verdant hue,
In the water's mirrored view.

Harmony in liquid form,
In each ripple, smiles warm,
Swirling, dancing, never mild,
In the brook, pure joy compiled.

Milton Keynes UK
Ingram Content Group UK Ltd.
UKHW020811210824
447217UK00007B/57